In loving memory of
Bryce Bradford

The Ballerina and The Bear

# The Brave Little Fighter

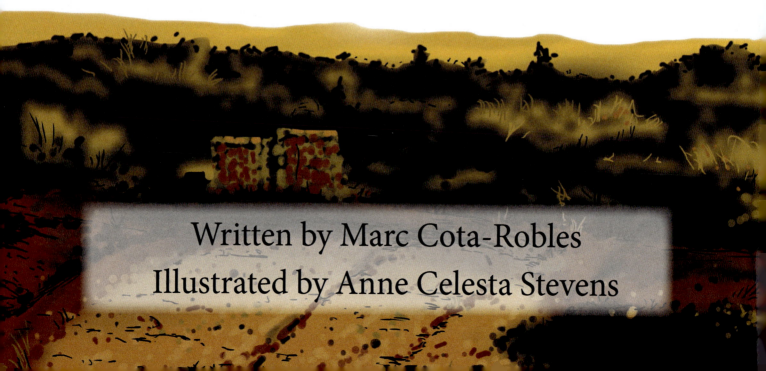

Written by Marc Cota-Robles

Illustrated by Anne Celesta Stevens

Copyright © 2020 by Ballerina and the Bear Publishing, LLC.

All Rights Reserved. No portion of this publication may be transmitted, reproduced, or stored in a retrieval system by any means including but not limited to, electronic, photocopy, recording, or any other form, without express written permission of the publisher. For information regarding permission please contact The Ballerina and the Bear Publishing, LLC.

Published in San Antonio, Texas, by The Ballerina and the Bear Publishing, LLC.
Text © 2020 Marc Cota-Robles
Illustrations © 2020 by Anne Celesta Stevens.

The Ballerina and the Bear titles may be purchased in bulk for educational, business, sales, promotional use, and fund-raising. For more information, please vist www.ballerinabearpublishing.com

ISBN-13: 978-1-949439-07-6

Printed in the United States of America

Presented to:

_____

From:

_____

Date:

_____

That joy and excitement,
it didn't last.
I was in trouble,
I needed help, fast!

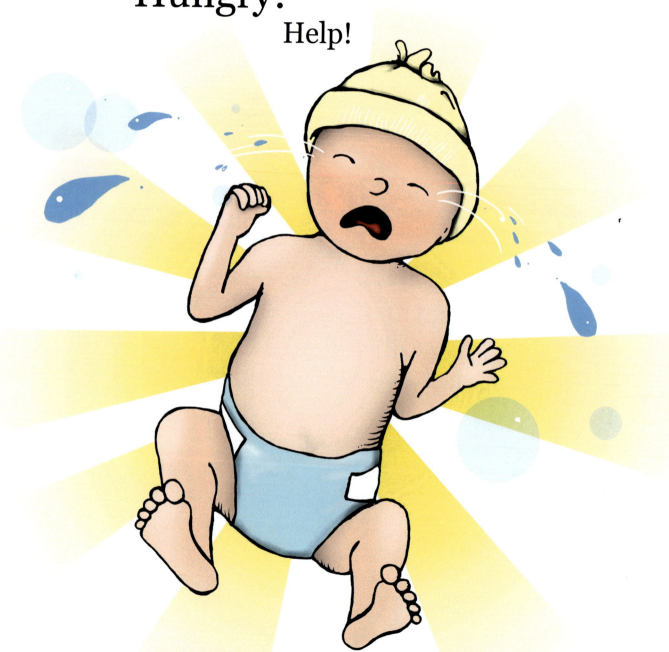

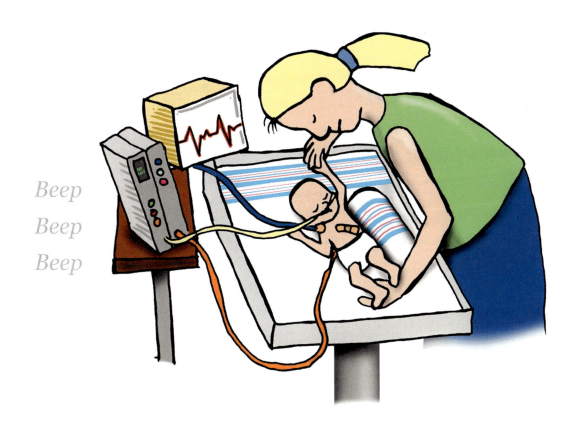

*Beep*

*Beep*

*Beep*

So tired.

So tired.

# Wow, what a first day!
My mommy would say,
I had big, scary challenges headed my way.

I didn't mind.
I'm a brave little fighter,
tougher than most you could find.

They took me home to a big brick house.
Mommy, plus daddy and me, made three.

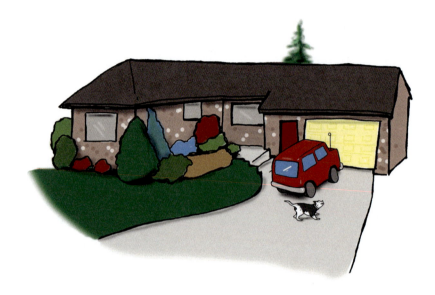

HEY! Who's he?!
He looks NOTHING like me!
"Surprise," said mommy, "in this home,
we have one more!"

He was grey and white - and spotted - and
had an extra set of legs… I counted four!

Some mommies,
they worry about big brothers like mine.
Not this mom.
Not me either.

For us, this brother was better than fine.
Together, we would spend most of our time.

*sniff*
*lick*
*lick*

Mommy told me at this home,
I would always be safe in.
Who was I to question?

We had a room where mommy and daddy
would make our beds in.

Away from that big brick house were other places we would stay.

Like the small hospital....

...and the BIG one ..

It felt like miles, planes and trains away!

This book is dedicated to my children - Mikey, Kobe, and Jojo. We all feel anger sometimes and that's normal. What makes the difference is how we manage it.

Copyright © Grow Grit Press LLC. 978-1-951056-06-3. All rights reserved. No part of this book may be reproduced in any form without permission in writing from the publisher. Please send bulk order requests to marynhin@gmail.com Printed and bound in the USA. First printing November 2019. GrowGrit.co

"Give it back!" screamed Angry Ninja.

His little sister had used his jumprope without asking and it made Angry Ninja furious.

Angry Ninja could feel his throat tighten, his heart beat faster, and his breathing start to get heavy.

He felt as if he was going to scream any second.

It wasn't fun being upset and having everyone mad at you. But Angry Ninja just didn't know how to control his emotions.

The two talked about it.

Positive Ninja explained, "Anger is normal. It's how you deal with it that makes a difference. There's something I do and it's super easy."

"I use the 1 + 3 + 10. I say 1 calm word like 'Relax'. You could say, 'Breathe'. Then, I take 3 slow, deep breaths. Finally, I count to 10," said Positive Ninja.

After I've calmed down, I add an 'I am _____' statement. Like if my sister broke my toy, I might say,

Afterwards, Angry Ninja went inside to get some chocolate cake his mom had made.

When he found out his sister ate the very last slice...

Angry Ninja said to himself, "Breathe."
He took 3 slow, deep breaths.

Breathe...

1, 2, 3...

Then, counted to 10.

A simple strategy to stay calm could become your secret weapon for managing anger.

Sign up for new Ninja book releases at GrowGrit.co

📷 @marynhin @GrowGrit
#NinjaLifeHacks

f  Mary Nhin    Grow Grit

▶ Grow Grit

Made in the USA
Coppell, TX
22 January 2020

Together, our family,
we had big plans.
"Move aside," I said,
"it's time to meet my fans!"
Wouldn't that be fun?
It was a dream,
reserved for a lucky one.

*I wonder what he is dreaming about?*

and bright sizzling sun.

Here, I breathe.
I take it all in.
When my time is up,
memories made here will be my win.

Mommy was sad.
Daddy, too.
There was a deep, dark secret
they felt -- they knew.

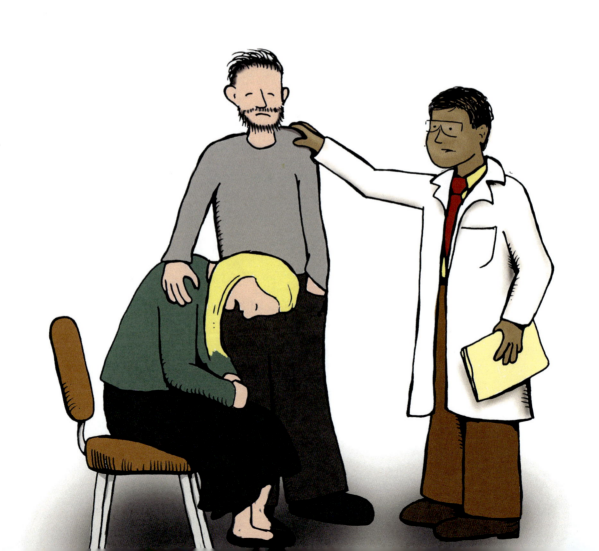

My dreams were dreams.
They don't always come true.

Tubes and tests.
Special flights.
I fought so hard, with all my might.

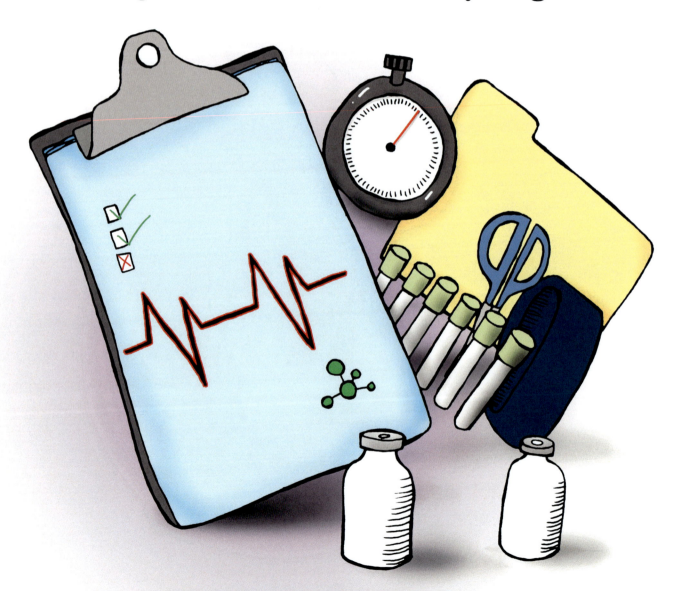

The day, it came.
Mommy, don't cry.
Daddy's still here.
I love you...goodbye.

# No time to question, get angry or fret...

# Wouldn't you say it's better we met?

Here on earth my heart was weak.
But in heaven, it's strong...
Up here, we can speak.

It's a place I will wait and you know it's true,
you did nothing wrong my mommy...

Bryce Bradford

Made in the USA
Coppell, TX
22 January 2020